Dedicated to all the terminally online workers of the world.

Copyright Joan Marie Arroyo Alcon – 2022

Prelude

I've been so far a leftist, an anarcho-communist, for over a year now. I think it should be near the first anniversary of my escape from the far right and my introduction to leftism and my trans non-binary identity. Even if my experience in the political left is still young for a bit, I think I got a solidified idea of what the basic moral principles of my ideology are.

I've been told by the authorities that I was probably the nicest of the bunch they had to detain. For a good reason: all this time I've been trying to make the world a better place, whether I believed in one ideology or another. I always wanted to feel empathy for my peers, however, the far-right has shown me that empathy has no place there. So I had to escape into the left, seeking to aid those who were truly oppressed, one way or the other. I knew I had limited resources to be able to aid the cause, limited economics from my monthly wage of around 500-600 euros, my reputation was probably near, if not completely, destroyed by hostile agents of psyops from the far right on all sides, given the circumstances in my past that I've been through, and still I had little to no platform to defend myself with. So I had to make out the most I could with that kind of resource.

Me, all alone, however, can't do proper shit. I am a noisemaker in a whole ocean of noisemakers, and it's barely audible from the rest. So, my best hope with this manifesto is that you can read it and understand why and how we can sort out the real injustices of this world with me. One tiny step at a time.

I don't want to be a leader, since vertical hierarchies are not my cup of tea, but all I want is to join the fight with my comrades and beat the shit out of fascists and capitalists and anything that stands in our way.

Chapter 1: On playing nice

First of all, the biggest key fundamental rule of my ideology is that being nice to the enemy is a weakness that the enemy can exploit and take advantage of.

In the capitalist or fascist system, we're all too accustomed to playing by their rules, playing their game, and abiding by their rules in every single aspect of the game: the discourse, the law, the ethics, the morality, etc. However, it has been demonstrated time and time again since centuries that this very game -which rules we're abiding by and which we're still playing to this day- is rigged. Every nook and cranny of this game, every rule of this game, every minacious part of this very fucking game is designed only to make our enemy win. To make the fascists and capitalists and those helping them achieve their goals simply win. And everyone else simply loses. Time and time again, we've played this game and lost every single time.

Fascists and capitalists, and also those who have been helping them win the game, have been using our kindness and the fact that we've been playing nice against us, taking advantage of it as a weakness of ours and as a weapon against us. There's no single doubt that it's not nice to be nice to our enemy and play by their rules. So there's only one thing we can do to our enemy; the capitalists, the fascists, and all those who help them and stand in our way of progress - and that is: being mean. Really, really bad.

But obviously, we cannot always need to break their laws and rules by committing brutal criminal acts, since they can also weaponize that to paint us in a bad way, and further cast us out of the whole Overton Window like we were the collective turd being flushed in the political toilet. Too many times, in their own game of capitalism and fascism, we've been getting in too much legal, social and economic trouble with protests, violence, looting, and other such criminal acts.

If we really wanted to break that system and trust me, this will do without them being able to put the blame on us and cast us out of the game and society, we have to use the tools that the system of fascism and capitalism gives us to be able to break that very system of fascism and capitalism.

These tools can be literally anything that they give us, directly or indirectly, especially there are two tools capitalism and fascism can give us either way: money and time. These two are essential, valuable resources within their system, and in the right hands, can do a lot of good for our cause. Money, for instance, can be given back to marginalized and poor voices so they can live decently with all their basic needs covered, redistributed, if you will, to the worker class. Capital, to say the least, can be redistributed amongst the worker class. Time, on the other hand, allows for the worker class to be able to use time in their advantage to dedicate themselves to working on real change. You can dedicate your spare time to being productive for the change that the world and society need.

There's also plenty of other tools that the system gives us as well, capitalist corporations, for instance, give us plenty of platforms, applications, and systems, especially in the digital age, where they're meant merely as consumer products where we're supposed to generate basic content for. However, these very platforms that corporations make, even the Silicon Valley giants like Facebook, Twitter, YouTube, Twitch, Amazon, etc. can be used to not just spread our ideology further into the whole world, but also to enact positive change, either through calls to action to our fellow comrades or either also by hacktivism.

The World Wide Web, considering things like WikiLeaks exist today in some form or another, has been a powerful tool to spread the ideas of our ideology in a sort of efficient way. Of course, we can't always rely on doing all the talk but no walk at all, like some cowardly grifters within the left, are doing, which I'll tackle in a later chapter, so it's not just about generating discourse about our current ideology and our cause, but also provoking the active action and activism that such discourse can cause. If you're committed to something, you can't just keep saying you're committed to doing it like if I already escaped from the far right, I can't really keep saying and talking all the time I've got out of there, but you also gotta show that through action, like I already show I'm committed to my new political cause by just doing the actual activism that I do (and let me note, of course, that not everybody knows what kind of activism I do not just online, but also offline, so they may judge me only by what I tend to show off online since I'm not usually socially open enough to showcase what kind of activism I do offline).

But back to my main point of this chapter: it's very obvious we can't rely on violence or criminal acts with these tools that the system gives us, but it's also obvious that we can't show a sign of weakness towards fascism and capitalism. We must use these tools in bad faith against our enemies who oppose our values and signs of progress, in a way that they can't exploit our weaknesses, but also in a way where they can't frame us badly enough we become ostracized from society itself.

The main reason why this works is that the blame on us using the tools capitalism and fascism give us to break them is on themselves. Even if capitalists and fascists gave us Molotov cocktails, we'd just throw those at them, and it'd

be their fault for giving those to us in the first
place. It's not really their brightest decision to
give us those tools in the first place, so they can't
be aware that we're giving those tools such
purpose, contrary to whatever purpose they give
those tools they've made. The right tool for them
in the wrong hands for them can make a whole
difference.

Chapter 2: On Fascism

Now that we got to the tools of real change, we must start recognizing our real enemies and who they really are. One of them is the fascists; the nazis, the conservatives, those who probably hold the same values as Adolf Fucking Hitler. You know who they are.

In my experience, I've been in the far right for around 4-5 years of my whole life, and, as I said, I found myself unable to find a single trace of empathy or decency there. True, my past haunts me, and I've done a little bit of similar horrible things that the far-right has done. Not to the point of committing violence, because even then, I found myself completely unable to harm a single flea, but still morally reprehensible acts that could not be justified and I obviously need to constantly remind and apologize for so I don't get to repeat them in the future.

However, this past experience of me in the far-right can help me and everyone further understand how the fascists and nazis work and can be weaponized against them as an example of what extent the fascists are willing to reach to meet their ends. These fascists, especially considering that ever since my young childhood, I've been trolled numerous times over and over again, have been committed abuse towards marginalized voices like mine, even neurodiverse voices like mine. Even to the point of taking advantage of mine or anyone else's neurodiversity to make us commit horrible acts for their personal gain. And that certainly isn't a good look for the fascists.

First of all, a thing that fascists tend to like a lot having is the sense of power over everyone else. I've felt it too before I entered the far-right; I've felt too weak to stand against the face of online bullying, so I joined the ranks of fascism in hopes I can gain strength or, at least, be able to defend myself against the incessant abuse. This didn't work for me, as my own diversity and neurodiversity have been weaponized by the rest of the far-right as if I was some sort of useful idiot. Not that nazis or fascists these days are more perfect than I am, far from it, but that sense of having power over so-called weaklings, like an alcoholic father who needs to beat his wife and kids to silence them and avoid them telling everyone else that the husband is abusive, has been used to silence marginalized voices and also those who tried to call out their wrongdoings, even from within the far-right itself.

Fascists are overreliant on that sort of imbalance of power to maintain a status quo that even the tamest of capitalists keep. The sad reality of fascism is that concepts like empathy or goodwill are not inherently convenient for the far-right narrative.

It is because of this that the fascists' and nazis' weakness is mainly their pure bad faith in everything.

In order to exploit this sort of weakness, we must act in a way where we don't platform fascism in any grounds of discourse, where we completely destroy their narrative and discourse not necessarily by violence, which is, again, gonna make the fascists be able to frame us into trouble, but by belittling and canceling every single bit of their discourse as if it was invalid in the public opinion arena. In the same way, some western countries have laws that criminalize their hate speech, we must completely deplatform any of their forms of hate speech, discourse, and ideas from the public sphere. Most of the platforms that the biggest corporations give us have tools with which we can completely eradicate these sorts of ideas from existence. At some point, they'll cry "censorship!" as if their ideas, within the excuse of total freedom of speech, are as valid as those of ours, but first of all, freedom of speech does not justify using speech to vulnerate the human rights of others; second of all, the capitalists and fascists have been also censoring us within the frame of freedom of speech, as a way of hypocrisy that they practice on the regular, and as long as our narrative doesn't fit with theirs; and third of all, freedom of speech does not imply freedom from consequences.

The problem with their speech, or rather, hate speech, is that it simply destroys, obliterates, and vulnerates the human rights of those who seem inferior to them. In the same way, they are willing to destroy and obliterate our speech so their speech remains uncontested. This is the ultimate abuse of fascism, it's all the way back to 1938.

For that reason, never ever platform a fascist on public discourse, no matter what. Platforming a fascist or giving them a resource to let them spread their hateful ideology is a cardinal sin that leads to further advancing their goals of vulnerating our rights for their own personal gain. This is a cardinal sin that a lot of leftists tend to erroneously do, in vain hopes they can invalidate their speech or narrative through debate or discourse, but again, this is playing nice on them. You never play nice on these people, because, as I said, they can weaponize that kindness of offering the fascists a platform as our weakness. We must show our strength in a way that we completely destroy their arguments, their reasoning, their speech, and their narrative, so it is not ever surfacing the public discourse.

Chapter 3: On the Capitalists

Another important enemy of ours is capitalists in any shape or form. They can take any disguise, whether they're corporate billionaires, cowardly democrats, moderates, centrists, anarcho-capitalists,… there's a whole infinite list of those who play in the capitalist team and I don't wanna go exhaustively detailing each and every one of them. But what they've been doing, as one of the major crimes of capitalism aside from exploiting the working class as we know it, is enabling fascism in every way conceivable.

One of the ways capitalists have been enabling fascism is that they've been doing little to nothing to stop the rise of fascism in any way. This has been one of the leading causes of the rise of the alt-right back in the online world years ago because the capitalist powers that be did little to no recourse to stop their pace. Even the democrats' compromise tactics have led recently to passing legislation that further hurt marginalized voices. The capitalists' fake façade of progressivism is often, in the words of Malcolm X, 7 inches forward but then 6 inches backward. That's not real progress. That's just the illusion of progress that masquerades the regressive trend towards fascism.

I cannot understand whether these acts of fake progressivism are out of pure self-interest or either out of laziness, but either way, capitalists have enabled this way the constant rapid pace of the advance of fascism towards the status quo.

Everyone who reads this is under my assumption also of understanding basic leftist theory, such as that of Karl Marx or Kropotkin, of understanding that the bourgeoisie is exploiting the working class and that we must seize the means of production as the working class. However, under neoliberalism, and under our current digital age, it's like capitalists have somehow normalized this power imbalance to the point of us being completely comfortable with it to the point of not doing anything about it because it's normal now. And with the whole pseudo-progressive narrative that capitalists tend to pull through into us, like the numerous times the Pride flag is merely turned into a bureaucratic action during a single month to generate LGBTQIA+ sales during that period of time, or the times a corporation pulls out a "solemn jpeg" to pretend they're condemning bigotry wherever it is from their organization, to appease marginalized voices; the people of color, the LGBTQIA+… the working class in general.

So it must be clear that these same goals of seizing the means of production from the bourgeoisie, into the working class, are kept the same. Except now, in the digital age, we must do this using the same platforms and tools that capitalists give us, whether it is social media, services, or products of any kind, to actually seize the means of production in any way possible, even to spread our ideology efficiently or to take action.

Chapter 4: On the cowardly false leftists

We must now understand the final enemy of
ours, the one that fascists and capitalists alike are
using to their advantage, and that is the people
who stand in our way against us from enacting
real change. You know who these people are;
those who call themselves "leftists" but do little
to nothing to help us or to stop capitalism and
fascism.

The inherent problem with the platforms and
tools that capitalism and fascism give us is that
these have the potential to corrupt our way of
being in any way possible. Social media is to
blame for this, and I don't think I need to explain
the whole neuroscience behind what drives
people into constantly chasing clout on social
media all the time no matter the cost or their
integrity. It's very easy to look at these tools and
what they can give us and be persuaded by the
tempting race towards personal success, fame, or
money (capital). However, it is extremely
dangerous to try to achieve such influence,
because of the potential of having us become our
own enemy in our pursuit of a bigger influence,
economic or social.

Many so-called "leftists" have tried using these tools for the better, but in their pursuit of enacting real change through these tools, they ended up being contaminated completely by the lure of easy money and fame, thus their constant clout chasing has driven them into greed, into behavior that disregards their integrity in favor of personal gain and profit.

In my recent year of experience as a fellow leftist comrade, I've been ostracized and kicked out from these false leftists' communities and environments, because they ended up listening to fascists who tried to get me deplatformed in hopes I can be gone from existence for them. These false leftists, contemporaries like Lance from The Serfs, Vaush, DemonMama… have been complicit in the sort of abuse and power imbalance that the fascists seek to exercise against me and others like me. They'd rather listen to the nonsense that an actual nazi like Britbong would tell them, and because of their cowardice and spinelessness in trying desperately to keep out any "inconvenient" people that might affect their public image, they've made me an outcast from their communities and personalities.

They can't be bothered to get to know me,
despite me telling them multiple times about my
past and my willingness to move past my
horrible fascist past or to understand what's my
current position ideologically and my reasoning
behind it. They just care about "not being
tainted" by the past that these fascists keep
haunting me with.

These false leftists are neither concerned about
enacting real change to a degree that they're too
busy circling around gossip dramatics in their
discourse. There's so much vain superficial
discourse within their debates, their streams, their
videos, their content, and their discourse; so
much that real activism and actual positive
change take second place within their constant
clout chasing. They often seem even as
distractions for people from ever enacting real
change, even if it's a really shitty charity stream
where everyone else but them raises money for a
cause. No. It's not just about money spent on
charities and non-profits who can do change. It's
also about protesting on the streets. It's also
about participating in activism. It's also about
defending the marginalized voices from outside

threats, like fascists or bigots. It's mainly also about getting up your ass and doing actual something.

The ineptitude of these false leftists, like The Serfs or Vaush, has led them into this attitude of "all talk, no walk" that curses the very leftist movement that we reside in. Mutual aid is reduced simply to a transaction where we only matter about getting something to gain for one of ourselves. Activism is turned into slacktivism that has no worth in being able to do the most minimal of positive change. Their words are embellished with the illusion that they're able to recruit or turn some of our enemies to our side, but the truth is: it's incredibly hard to convince a fascist or a capitalist, in the ground of debate or in any ground in general, to turn to our side. Because fascists and capitalists are so deeply rooted in their shitty ideology that, unless a real miracle happens, they are impossible to pull out from.

And more importantly, this is not just about me. These fake leftists' willingness to cave into the demands of fascists like the already mentioned

Britbong or anyone else will lead any of us who dare speak this truth into being ostracized from this horde of false leftists. Maybe then one can see the truth behind their masks.

Chapter 5: On the ex-fascists and those seeking reform

I can't honestly lie about my intentions: I've been seeking to reform from my incredibly horrible past ever since that epiphany of becoming a leftist hit me. And like I said, this past experience as a member of the far-right can be weaponized by us against the fascists and capitalists themselves.

Of course, there will be those like me who, after any given circumstance, will be seeking to reform and also escape from the far-right. Most of the leftist communities will treat them with skepticism, at least. The false leftists will not allow them within because they want to keep their positive image intact. However, what they don't realize is the potential of these ex-nazis and ex-fascists to show us how the far-right operates and how we can weaponize their past experiences against actual fascism.

In the case that someone, as an ex-nazi, has been clearly showcasing the willingness and the capability of enacting real positive change, we must show them empathy, because maybe they have been the oppressors, the perpetrators of horrible acts, but in the end, they're also the victims of an ideology that's broken and immoral enough to manipulate them into doing horrible things. Not only they'll have to eventually have justice served into them if such horrible acts include acts of violence, but we must help them also to see how horrible those acts were, helping them smoothly transition from the far-right into our movement, and make them never come back into those acts and that ideology. Because in the end, they're equally human beings like us, to a degree or another.

it's understandable that not everyone who appears to be reforming from the far-right is actually reforming from the far-right, thus we must be careful with this, but we can at least hope that, if given the chance to reform a past fascist into a better person, we must use this chance to give them a second chance and make them join our movement. They must understand the values that we strive for; the values of empathy, respect, mutual aid, and so on. It's not an easy task; I, myself, still struggle to transition in a lesser way given how hard is to deprogram someone from the far-right's narrative; but with the right attitude, the right tools, the right resources, and the right education we can turn these ex-nazis into comrades that can help us fight against fascism and capitalism, weaponizing their past against fascism and capitalism.

Understanding how fascism and capitalism work is essential to our constant struggle. We must not only use the right weapons and tools to fight against the evils of fascism and capitalism, but we must also have the knowledge to know how to fight them appropriately. Without getting too much into trouble, without playing too nice, without compromising, and without fail.

TERMINALLY ONLINE WORKERS OF THE WORLD, UNITE!

Content Index